The Power of 4 in Your Marriage
"Faith, Trust, Humility, Love"

Jerome & Ivy Moore

DEDICATION

To my friend, partner, and Proverbs 31 wife, Ivy,
a woman who has my heart. A Prayer warrior. The word
of God says that when a man finds a wife he finds a good
thing and receives favor with God. When He gave me you
it was with faith, trust, humility, and love. You always kept
pushing and keeping me motivated all these years of
marriage.

Your continued support through all that we have gone
through; and understanding of what it is to be a man.
To my friend, partner, and Man of integrity, Jerome. You
exemplify what a man is; it is not money, cars, or material
wealth but the love of God. Thanks for continuing to cover
me as your wife in prayer, and having the strength to
uphold in tough times and all that we have been through.
To our children Eric and Monesha; to whom we continue
to love, cherish, and support all the days of our life. You
are the best children God created. May we leave a legacy
for your children and children's' children. All giving thanks,
glory and honor to our Lord and Savior Jesus Christ.

Acknowledgments

Sincere appreciation is expressed to those whom we have coached in various ways in the preparation of our 2nd book. As you begin to heal and strengthen your relationship with God you too will experience how to have more faith, trust, humility, and love. Thanks to the marriages and individuals that have asked the tough questions and given us more encouragement, strength, grace and motivation of writing this book. Gratitude is acknowledged to our Lord and Savior Jesus Christ & many others who have covered us in prayer.

CONTENTS

1   Faith   Pg 1

2   Trust   Pg 26

3   Humility   Pg 36

4   Love   Pg 46

CHAPTER 1

FAITH

"Now faith is the substance of things hoped for, the evidence of things not seen" Hebrews 11:1 NKJV

F-Favor- v8 God, you designed my body. You made me. But now you attack me. v9 You made me from the earth, like a pot. Soon my body will die, and it will become dust again. v10 As a man makes cheese from milk, you made my body. v11 You provided skin to cover my body. And you made bones to join my body's parts together. v12 You caused my body to live. You were kind to me. You protected my spirit. *Job 10:12*

Job could see that God designed the human body. And Job could see that this was not a simple task. God acted carefully when he made Job's body. God did not cause Job to live by accident. Rather, God showed great kindness to Job. These facts made Job's problem seem even stranger. Surely, God would not cruelly destroy the person that he made so carefully.

A-Arise
v1 'Rise, Jerusalem, and shine like the sun! The glory of the Lord is shining on you! *Isaiah 60:1*
The Lord is speaking to 'Jerusalem'. 'Jerusalem' refers to both the city and its inhabitants. So, through this whole

chapter, 'you' means both the city and its inhabitants. 'Rise' means 'get up to act'. The action is 'to shine'. That is, the people are to express bright hope for their future, because of God's firm promises.

When dawn comes in the East, it appears very quickly. The sudden sunshine on the white rock of the Temple is a powerful contrast with the earlier black night. This provides a word picture of the experience of Jerusalem and its inhabitants. The Lord will suddenly act. He will free the exiles from their hopeless darkness (despair) in Babylon. And he will bring them home to Jerusalem.

I-Instruct- v8 I will tell you the way,
I will teach you where you must go.
My eye will be your guide. ***Psalm 32:8***

David probably wrote Psalm 32 after he had slept with Bathsheba. She was the wife of Uriah. David sent Uriah to die in battle. Then David married Bathsheba. For a while he did not ask God to forgive him. As a result he was very unhappy. Then he told God that he was sorry. God forgave him. David became happy again. Christians have a special word for being sorry for their sins. The word is repentance. There are 7 Repentance Psalms. The others are 6,38 51,102, 130 and 143.

Verses 8 – 9: These words are not David speaking to us. They are God speaking to us. It is a special promise of God. God will always show us what to do if we ask him. We must not be like animals, like the horse and the mule. We must be like people that God can talk to.

T-Transformed

v1 Brothers and sisters, God has shown you his kindness. Therefore I am appealing to you. Offer your bodies to him as a sacrifice that is alive. Your gift will please God greatly. This is true spiritual worship. v2 Do not live any longer in the way that this world lives. ***Romans 12:1-2*** Change completely the way that you think. Then you will be able to test what God wants. You will discover that God's plan is good and acceptable. It is perfect. Paul appeals to all the Christians in Rome. God has shown his great love to them all. So they should be grateful. If they have the right attitude to God, then they will think rightly about themselves. This will make a difference to their relationships with other people. Paul uses the idea of a priest who offers a sacrifice. The sacrifice had to be a perfect animal. Then it would please God (Leviticus 1:3, 9).

Christians must offer their bodies as a sacrifice to God. Paul is not writing about death here. He is explaining how Christians should live their lives in this world. They should try to use every part of their bodies in a manner that pleases God. They will use their feet. They will go where God wants them to go. They will use their hands to give practical help to other people. With their ears, they will listen to other people's problems. With their mouths, they will speak to encourage other people and to tell them the good news about Christ. The right use of the body will be like the perfect sacrifice that pleased God. Their worship would not just be a ceremony. This is the right kind of worship. It is spiritual. It is the worship that God asks for.
 Christians must also change the way that they think. The word 'change' is the same word that describes the change in Jesus' body. Jesus changed when he showed his glory to

the three apostles (Mark 9:2). It is easy for people to copy
what other people do. But Christians should not copy
everything that people in the world do. Christians belong to
God's world. So they should behave in a different way
from people who are not Christians.
What Christians think will affect what they do. Christians
will think differently about the use of money. Christians
will remember that money belongs to God. So they will try
not to waste it or to use it selfishly. They will have a
different opinion about sex. They will make careful choices
about what they read. They will select carefully what they
watch on television. The Holy Spirit will guide Christians as
they try to please God. They will want to obey God, so that
they can 'reflect the Lord's glory. Then they will continue
to change and to be like him' (2 Corinthians 3:18).

H-healed- v13 If anyone among you is in trouble, that
person should pray to God. If anyone among you is
cheerful, that one should sing praises to God. v14 If one of
you is sick, let him ask for the church elders to come. They
will put oil on the sick person, and pray in the name of the
Lord. v15 The prayer offered in faith will make the sick
person well. The Lord will heal that person. And he will
forgive any sins that he or she has done. v16 So then,
confess your sins to one another. Pray for one another, that
the Lord will heal you. God does powerful things when a
good person asks him.. *James 5:13-16*

If anyone is in trouble, that person should pray to God.
The answer to that prayer may not remove the problem.
But it will give help and strength to be able to live through
the trouble. Those who are cheerful (who feel good) should
praise God. They should sing psalms or praises to God.
James is reminding his readers to turn to God in good

times as well as bad. Prayer and praise are important parts in the lives of Christians.

When they are ill, they should ask the elders to come and pray with them. The elders are the leaders and pastors of the church. They can pray and believe that God will answer them. When the elders have come, they will pray over the sick person. They will put oil on that person in the name of the Lord. This is a request for God to act, because he is the source of all healing. In those days, people used oil as a medicine. They put oil into injuries to clean them and to aid healing. As an example of this, see Luke 10:34. The Good Samaritan poured oil into the injuries of the man whom the thieves had attacked. When Jesus sent the apostles out to preach, they put oil on the sick people and healed them (Mark 6:13). It could be then, that here oil is a sign of healing. The cure is not by means of the oil but by the power of the Lord.

Those who pray with the sick person must believe. They must believe that God will answer their prayers. They must be confident that God will heal. It is the prayer with faith that God uses. It is prayer, not the oil, that leads to the healing of the sick person. In answer to the prayer, God will make the sick person well again. If sin was the cause of the illness, God will forgive that sin. 'If' makes it clear that not all illness comes from sin. More often than not sin is not the direct cause of it.

It is not only the elders and the sick person who should pray. All the Christians should pray for one another. They should confess their sins to one another. They must pray for one another that God may heal them. As they confess their faults and pray for one another, God makes them clean. He forgives them and they forgive one another. Those whom God forgives he considers to be righteous persons. When they pray to God, he will hear them. God does great things in answer to their prayers.

God and his word should be more important to us than anything else is. Our money and our good clothes do not make him happy. The good things that we do are important to him. And the kind words that we speak are important to him too. He wants us to be good to our workers, good to our sisters and brothers, good to our cousins, good to our spouses, good to our mother and father. It makes God happy when rich people give money to help poor people.

We've all heard; faith is the substance of things hoped for, the evidence of things not seen."But what does that mean to you? Has it just become a word without definition? Or is "Faith" a lifestyle you strive for? We hear all around us today; prayers aren't answered because we lack faith." That's only partially true. Just because God heals one person of cancer, doesn't mean he will do the same for you. That doesn't always mean you lack faith. His plan for you is different than anyone else. God is the same yesterday, today and forever. But His plan for each one of us is different. You can't put God in a box, expecting Him to perform the same way each time, or on demand. No amount of seed offerings, prayer vigils or fasting can change God's plan.

We hear so many times; God did it for me, He'll do it for you. The correct statement would be, God did it for me, He could do it for you. But we will never know, if we lack the faith to believe. You ask and do not receive, because you ask amiss, that you may spend it on your pleasures." James 4:3 If you believe; the faith of a mustard seed can move a mountain, and you have mountain moving faith then you have faith. But can you act on it? Can you give your problems to Jesus and leave them there? Or do you drag them back, clinging to them, in fear? "Therefore submit to God. Resist the devil and he will flee from you. Draw near to God and He will draw near to you. Cleanse your hands, you sinners; and purify your hearts, you are double-minded. Lament and mourn and weep! Let your laughter be turned to mourning and your joy to gloom. Humble yourselves in the sight of the Lord, and He will lift you up. James 4:7-10. We've heard so many people cry out; but my prayers aren't being answered, it's not meant to be but have you surrendered it all? Is your life totally His? Or are you keeping one foot in the world? Afraid? Filled with fear or apprehension. Fear is a tool of the devil, don't let him use it on you. An unpleasant emotion caused by the belief that someone or something is dangerous, likely to cause pain, or a threat. However, fear in itself, is a natural instinct that pertains to all human beings. On its good side, fear is what keeps us from doing things which could place us in danger, so it's not all bad.

However, when fear stops you from doing something you would like to be able to do, it's time to evaluate your inner belief system and make some adjustments. **A small change that improves something or makes it work better.** It's time to empower yourself to go forth with self-confidence, strength, and conviction. If you are fearful, it is most likely over something that you're wondering about in the tomorrows or something you're reflecting on from the yesterdays. Yesterday and tomorrow only rob you of today by creating anxiety and anguish. Whatever was, is gone and whatever might be, is greatly affected by the right here and now, and you can change that minute by minute. The here and now is where you have your greatest capacity to make changes and create new tomorrows in your marriage. Even if you're in the process of performing an action which is fearful to you, in the moment that you begin the action, you have the power to hold your focus more on the action that you are performing, than on the fear of it. **Remember, God is not the author of confusion. He brings light into the darkness, and order into chaos. Sometimes God is looking for a group of people, as in a organization, church, a community, leadership, a country, or even your marriage to have faith, not just the individual.**

"Who through faith subdued kingdoms, wrought righteousness, obtained promises, stopped the mouths of lions. Quenched the violence of fire, escaped the edge of the sword, out of weakness were made strong, waxed valiant in fight, turned to flight the armies of the aliens." *Hebrews 11:33-34.*

Whose will is it that you are following? Your own or God's? Are you in tune with His word? Do you know His desire for you? It does not mean that you are less godly than those who seemingly do not and it also does not mean that you need to obtain a certain level of holiness before that desire is allowed or granted. Marriage is always a gift. God doesn't do works-righteousness, not in salvation and not in matrimony. If you are not yet married but desire to be, place your desire in the hands of the Father who, because of Jesus, delights to give good gifts to his children. Marriage can become an idol, so as we suggests, ask God to give you a vision for the sacrifice and commitment required and run to God who gives grace and forgiveness. Even still, although in some people it does not feel right, ask him for that gift. When your heart aches from not yet having received the good gift that you desire, go to him and take hold of his promises. Marriage is a good desire and God is a good God who is worthy of our trust. Make sure you continue to long or hope for. Do you listen?

"So then faith comes by hearing, and hearing by the Word of God. *Romans 10:17*

When you study His word, follow His teachings, obey His commands, and listen with your heart. That is the beginning, now step out, and act in faith.

"Show me your faith without your works, and I will show you my faith by my works.*" James 2:18*

Now, do you think your road will always be smooth? Everything bright and sunny? No! "My brethern, count it all joy when you fall into various trials, knowing that the testing of your faith produces patience.*" James 1:2-3*

How can we know that our faith is nonproductive in marriage ? So after Abram had been living in Canaan ten years, Sarai his wife took her Egyptian maidservant Hagar and gave her to her husband to be his wife. *(Genesis 16:3)*

Nonproductive Faith in marriage attempts to anticipate God's plan. Sarai took matters into her own hands by giving Hagar to Abram. Like Abram she had trouble believing God's promise that was apparently directed specifically toward Abram and Sarai. Out of this lack of faith came a series of problems. This invariably happens when we take over for God, trying to make his promise come true through efforts that are not in line with his specific directions. Time was the greatest test of Abram and Sarai's willingness to let God work in their lives. Sometimes we too must simply wait. What does waiting mean to you? To us it is simply a period during which one waits; a pause or delay. When we ask God for something and have to wait, it is a temptation to take matters into our own hands and interfere with God's plans. As the Egyptian army approached, the people of Israel saw them far in the distance, speeding after them, and they were terribly frightened and cried out to the Lord to help them. And they turned against Moses, whining, "Have you brought us out here to die in the desert because there were not enough graves for us in Egypt? Why did you make us leave Egypt?" *Exodus 14:10-11*

Nonproductive Faith in marriage is marked by a lack of trust in God. Do you trust Him? Trapped against the sea, the Israelites faced the Egyptian army sweeping in for the kill. The Israelites thought they were doomed. After watching God's powerful hand deliver them from Egypt, their only response was fear, whining, and despair. Where was their trust in God? Israel had to learn from repeated experience that God was able to provide for them. God has preserved these examples in the Bible so that we can learn to trust him the first time and all the time. By focusing on God's faithfulness in the past we can face crises with confidence rather than with fear and complaining. We should be Producing plenty of fruit in keeping with repentance. *(Matthew 3:8)*

Nonproductive Faith in marriage is marked by an unchanged life. Marked meaning singled out for notice or especially for a dire fate. God's message hasn't, doesn't and will never be changed. People will be judged for their unproductive lives. God calls us to be active in our obedience. John compared people who claim they believe in God but don't live for him to unproductive trees that will be cut down. Marriages should be fruitful. A vineyard owner was disappointed for three years in succession and wanted to cut the useless fig-tree down. It was a waste of space! Her farm manager, on the other hand, wanted to give it another chance. She knew that the fig-tree had the potential to produce figs. It wasn't an oak-tree but a fig-tree and it was in the nature of fig-trees to produce figs. It is very important to recognize the potential of your mate. The manager of the fig-tree decided to stir up its roots. The manager thought if she dug around the fig-tree it might be stimulated into fruitfulness. Sometimes if a failing shrub is dug up and replanted it thrives. We are not experts in fig-trees and cannot tell if stirring up the roots is likely to have much effect but the strategy sure helps.

Roots keep a tree secure. If the roots are stirred up it threatens the trees security. Sometimes God uses adversity disappointments, dislocations and disruptions to make us less secure and produce fruitfulness.

Roots keep a tree content. The fig takes up water and nutrients through the roots. If its roots are stirred up it is less content.

Complacency and self-satisfaction keep many marriages from delivering what God wants. Jesus stirred up the Pharisees during his public ministry. They were pleased with themselves as they were and self-righteous. The Pharisees trusted to their Jewish and visible adherence to the Law of Moses. Jesus attacked the Pharisees not just to make them feel bad but in the hope that they would examine themselves and change.

Marriages sometimes need a good coach to stir up the pot. Marriages must be told to get their priorities right. It is more important to cover your spouse in prayer than watch TV, or weed the garden.. Marriages do not like being stirred up any more than the Pharisees. We know what they did to Jesus! Not many marriages get crucified - they just leave.

Just as a fruit tree is expected to bear fruit, God's people should produce a crop of good deeds and seeds. God has no use for people who call themselves believers but do nothing about it. Like many people in John's day who were God's people in name only, we are of no value if we are believers in name only. If others can't see our faith in the way we treat them, we may not be God's people at all. To be productive for God, we must obey his teachings, resist temptation, actively serve and help others, and share our faith. How productive are you for God, other marriages or people? Are you bearing fruit? But I will come, and soon, if the Lord will let me, and then I'll find out whether these proud men are just big talkers or whether they really have God's power. *1 Corinthians 4:19*

Nonproductive Faith in marriage seldom goes beyond words. Some people talk a lot about faith, but that's all it is—talk. They may know all the right words to say, but their lives don't reflect God's power. Paul says that the kingdom of God is to be lived, not just discussed. Discussed meaning to consider or examine by argument, comment, talk over or write down. There is a big difference between knowing the right words and living them out. Don't be content to have the right answers about Christ. Let your life show that God's power is really working in you. How can we know that our faith is lacking in our marriage? Then Peter called to him: "Sir, if it is really you, tell me to come over to you, walking on the water." *(Matthew 14:28)*

A Lack in faith in marriage tends to lack endurance. We are instructed by God in His word to cultivate endurance in our walk with Him. Hebrews 10:36 admonishes, "You have need of endurance, so that when you have done the will of God, you may receive what was promised." As Believers we have "need of endurance" to assure that we receive all of God's promises. In Luke 21:19 it is Jesus Himself who says, "…by your endurance you will gain your lives (souls)". The context there is the persecution, suffering and adversity one faces as a couple. We want the promises of God – we understand there is a cost – we long to gain our souls by the will of Christ. So, how can we begin to cultivate endurance in our lives?

Most of us dwell somewhere between the extremes of "Woe is me…." and "Look at me…" The first extreme ("Woe is me…") is where we isolate ourselves and sulk; feeling sorry for ourselves until someone eventually acknowledges us. The second extreme ("Look at me…") is where we become bitter and angry; murmuring and complaining to our spouse until they eventually acknowledges us. Either way the end result is a let down.

James says we ought to face the trials of life with an attitude of joyfulness. The attitude James is directing us to have is often misinterpreted as happiness. Joy and happiness are not synonyms. Happiness is typically based on what's currently happening to me or around me. It is the feeling I get when all my expectations are met. Its opposite, of course, is sadness which is the feeling I get when things don't go the way I expect them. "I am so happy!" WHY? "Well, because my spouse bought me flowers. "I am sad" WHY? "Because they never buy me flowers.

James isn't instructing us to face cancer or the loss of a loved one with a happy smile on our faces. He is, however, asking us to consider (count or reckon) our adversities by an attitude of calm delight. You see, joy is not circumstantial like happiness. It is a mindset which rests upon real knowledge and a firm understanding rather than what is happening to us or around us. A marriage can face a difficult trial with a calm delight based upon the knowledge that their faith will be strengthened and completed. This point is easy to dismiss if our attitude is wrong about suffering – but then, what are we left with?

James is asking us to 'reckon' our trials as opportunities for spiritual growth. Can we do it? Can we rise to the challenges we face in our walk of faith? Will we be beaten further and further down by them?

Hebrews 12:7-11 (NASB) "It is for discipline that you endure; God deals with you as with sons; for what son is there whom {his} father does not discipline? But if you are without discipline, of which all have become partakers, then you are illegitimate children and not sons. Furthermore, we had earthly fathers to discipline us, and we respected them; shall we not much rather be subject to the Father of spirits, and live? For they disciplined us for a short time as seemed best to them, but He disciplines us for our good, so that we may share His holiness. All discipline for the moment seems not to be joyful, but sorrowful; yet to those who have been trained by it, afterwards it yields the peaceful fruit of righteousness."

Discipline has almost become an offensive word in our marriages. At the very least, it is a sensitive issue. Some of us had earthly fathers that knew how to discipline us. Their discipline kept us safe and helped us to grow as human beings. Some of us, on the other hand, had earthly fathers who did what seemed best to them, leaving us feeling ashamed and without worth.

We realize it may be difficult for some of you, but try your best not to let your earthly experience jade your concept of what God has in store for you. His discipline is a source of the endurance you need to be assured of His promises and to gain your very souls.

There are times in life when we may become complacent about internal weaknesses and frailties in our faith. Maybe some grudge or guilt we're carrying needs releasing but we've harbored it so long we lack the will to let it go. Perhaps we're holding too tightly to some worldly attitude and we lack the wisdom and spiritual insight to gain the heavenly perspective. Whatever the reason may be, it seems that there are times in our lives when our Father applies some heat and pressure on us, for our own good. These times are often characterized by feelings of discomfort, pain and even sorrow. The result, however, is that we gain endurance; we reflect God's holiness in a better way; and ultimately, the peaceful fruit of righteousness is produced in our lives.

If we want to begin to cultivate endurance in our marriage then we must begin to change our attitude towards suffering and train ourselves to yield to the loving discipline of our Father in heaven. In future books, we will look at other areas where we might begin to cultivate endurance in our marriage lives.

Remember, Peter was not putting Jesus to the test, something we are told not to do **(Matthew 4:7)**. Instead he was the only one in the boat to react in faith. His impulsive request led him to experience a rather unusual demonstration of God's power. Peter started to sink because he took his eyes off Jesus and focused on the high waves around him. His faith wavered when he realized what he was doing. We may not walk on water, but we do walk through tough situations. If we focus on the waves of difficult circumstances around us without looking to Jesus for help, we too may despair and sink. To maintain your faith when situations are difficult, keep your eyes on Jesus' power rather than on your inadequacies.

A Lack of faith in marriage often falters. Although we start out with good intentions, sometimes our faith falters. This doesn't necessarily mean we have failed. When Peter's faith faltered, he reached out to Christ, the only one who could help. He was afraid, but he still looked to Christ. When you are apprehensive about the troubles around you and doubt Christ's presence or ability to help, you must remember that he is the only one who can really help. However, Peter ran to the tomb to look. Stooping, he peered in and saw the empty linen wrappings; and then he went back home again, wondering what had happened. **(Luke 24:12)**

A Lack of faith in marriage is a part of the process of belief. People who hear about the resurrection for the first time may need time before they can comprehend this amazing story. Like the disciples, they may pass through stages of belief. At first, they may think it is a non sense, impossible, and incapable to believe. Like Peter, they may check out the facts but still be puzzled and objectionable about what happened. Only when they encounter Jesus personally will they be able to accept the fact of the resurrection. Then, as they commit themselves to Jesus and devote their lives to serving him, and their marriage will they begin fully to understand the reality of his presence with them. The father instantly replied, "I do have faith; oh, help me to have more!" **(Mark 9:24)**

A lack of faith in marriage can become strong faith with God's help. The attitude of trust and confidence that the Bible calls belief or faith **(Hebrews 11:1-6)** is not something we can obtain without help. Faith is a gift from God **(Ephesians 2:8-9)**. No matter how much faith we have, we never reach the point of being self-sufficient. Faith is not stored away like money in the bank. Growing in faith is a constant process of daily renewing our trust in Jesus. Give a warm welcome to any brother who wants to join you, even though he lacks faith. Don't criticize him for having different ideas from yours about what is right and wrong. **(Romans 14:1)**

Marriages with a lack of faith need to recognize their limitations or boundaries. Who is weak in faith and who is strong? We are all weak in some areas and strong in others. Our faith is strong if we can survive contact with sinners without falling into their patterns. It is a lack of faith if we must avoid certain activities, people, or places in order to protect our spiritual life. It is important to take a self-inventory in order to find out our strengths and weaknesses in marriage. In areas of strength, we should not fear being defiled by the world; rather we should go and serve God. In areas of faithlessness, we need to be cautious. If we have strong faith but shelter it, we are not doing Christ's work in the world or to our spouse. Whenever in doubt, we should ask, "Can I do that without sinning?

Can I influence others for good, rather than being influenced by them?" How can we know our faith is effectual in marriage? One day the apostles said to the Lord, "We need more faith; tell us how to get it." **(Luke 17:5)** Effectual faith depends on God. The disciples' request was genuine; they wanted the faith necessary for radical forgiveness. But Jesus didn't directly answer their question because the amount of faith is not as important as its genuineness and honesty. What is faith? It is total dependence on God and a willingness to do his will. Faith is not something we use to put on a show for others. It is complete and humble obedience to God's will, readiness to do whatever he calls us to do. The amount of faith isn't as important as the right kind of faith—faith in our all-powerful God.

Faith in marriage is more concerned with its life than its size. A mustard seed is small, but it is alive and growing. Like a tiny seed, a small amount of genuine faith in God will take root and grow in time. Almost invisible at first, it will begin to spread, first under the ground and then visibly. Although each change will be gradual and imperceptible, soon this faith will have produced major results that will uproot and destroy competing loyalties. We don't need more faith; a tiny seed of faith is enough, if it is alive and growing. So now, since we have been made right in God's sight by faith in his promises, we can have real peace with him because of what Jesus Christ our Lord has done for us. **(Romans 5:1)**

Faith in marriage rests on what Christ has done. As Paul states clearly in **1 Corinthians 13:13**, faith, hope, and love are at the heart of the Believers life. Our relationship with God begins with faith, which helps us realize that we are delivered from our past by Christ's death. Hope grows as we learn all that God has in mind for us; it gives us the promise of the future. And God's love fills our life and gives us the ability to reach out to others. And those whose faith has made them good in God's sight must live by faith, trusting him in everything. Otherwise, if they shrink back, God will have no pleasure in them. **(Hebrews 10:38)**

Faith in marriage grows under pressure. Pressure is the amount of force the weight or force that is produced when something presses or pushes against something else. Pressure is like that olive being pressed in the drum and making the oil. Most of the fatty acids in olives and olive oil are mono-unsaturated. Mono-unsaturated fatty acids do not contain cholesterol. Therefore, olive oil does not raise cholesterol levels but instead keeps them under control. God had a reason for it. Our perfection, strength, and growth come through pressures we face each and every day. Pressure does not make you great. Pressure does not make you strong. It's how you act in the pressure that makes you strong. It's the Word you use in the pressure that makes you strong. It's the weapons you use in that pressure that make you strong. Some people say, "Tribulations make you strong." Satan is the author of all

19

the tribulations and trials that come our way. If tribulation makes you strong, then Satan is the author of our strength. That's not true. That's blasphemy. Satan is the author of tribulations. He wants to destroy us. God wants us to use His weapons from His Word to overcome those tribulations that come against us. Overcoming tribulation is how we become strong and mature.

The Hebrews encourages believers to persevere in their Christian faith and conduct when facing persecution and pressure. We don't usually think of suffering as good for us, but it can build our character and our patience. During times of great stress, we may feel God's presence more clearly and find help from Believers we never thought would care. Knowing that Jesus is with us in our suffering and that he will return one day to put an end to all pain, helps us grow in our faith and our relationship with him (**Romans 5:3-5).**

Faith in marriage becomes stronger through endurance. We encourage you not to abandon your faith in times of persecution, but to show by your endurance that your faith is real. Faith means resting in what Christ has done for us in the past, but it also means hoping for what he will do for us in the future **(see Romans 8:12-25;Galatians 3:10-13)**.

What is faith? It is the confident assurance that something we want is going to happen. It is the certainty that what we hope for is waiting for us, even though we cannot see it up ahead. **(Hebrews 11:1)**

Faith in marriage is hopeful anticipation. Do you remember how you felt when you first got engaged? You were excited and anxious. You knew you would certainly receive gifts, and a honeymoon to somewhere in the world. But some things would be a surprise. Weddings combine assurance and anticipation, and so does faith! Faith is the conviction based on past experience that God's new and fresh anticipation will surely be ours.

He promised He would be with you. "Many are the afflictions of the righteous, but the Lord delivers him out of them all." He promised us we'll be more than conquerors, but keep in mind, a conqueror goes to battle. To be more than a conqueror requires going into battle, but we come back victorious every single time. Just as Jesus, Paul, and Peter faced afflictions, we face afflictions. This verse says that born again people are not exempt from problems. Even we groan within ourselves waiting for the adoption that is the redemption of our body. Until the time we either receive a resurrection body or we die, we are going to be under the pressures and anticipation of this world, and trials and troubles will come against us.

Our desire is to have a good rapport with the world. We want to have good rapport with the apostle, the community and others in positions of authority or influence. It's nice to have it, and yes, God does give favor. Jesus increased in favor with God and man. But don't build your life on favor with people. Build your life on favor with God, because your favor with God will never change, but your favor with the world will change from minute to minute and day to day. One minute they like you; the next minute they despise you. However, God always has His favor toward you. You follow after Him and the favor of men will result, but you can't build your life on the favor of men. Even Jesus was loved at times and hated at times. Paul was loved at times and hated at times. The same happened to the other disciples. Even though Jesus increased in stature and in favor with God and man, the favor with man would change from day to day. Again, we groan.

Effectual faith in marriage is quiet certainty. Two words describe faith: That it is sure and it is certain. Sure and Certain meaning free from doubt as to the reliability, confident, and convinced. These two qualities need a secure beginning and ending point. The beginning point of faith is believing in God's character—he is who he says. The end point is believing in God's promises; he will do what he says. When we believe that God will fulfill his promises even though we don't see those promises materializing yet, we demonstrate true faith **(John 20:24-31)**.

Yes, sometimes weeks and months are hard. That saying "when it rains, it pours" seemed like it was written just for us. We often times tell people that saying is true but it is also true of blessings. Remember, Ruth when she gleaned in the fields and Boaz took notice of her and she became his wife. God can and will rain blessings on our lives at times. We feel sometime's as if one of the biggest blessings in our life could be taken from us at any moment. Our vehicle was not cooperating and we finally got the engine rebuilt and still having oil pressure issues but at least it was running. We went to run some errands and on the way back the car went out.....right before a red light! We were screaming inside and yet we knew if we turned it off we were stuck as we could not push start it. If the clutch is not pushed in; it will not start period. We got through the first light as there was very little traffic and we were turning right. Okay, two more stop lights, a railroad crossing, a stop sign and about 2 miles to the house. Our mind remembered every wide place in the road directly before a stop light or stop sign. We only had to pull off and circle for one red light. Next is the gate at the house. Oh boy! We have to tell you, it was rather comical! No injuries, just another trial and test from the Lord. As we went to bed that night and read the word as usual and when we saw "Rejoice in the Lord always, again I say rejoice" we cried out to God. "Even when it seems like trials and tribulations; coming from every direction. He impressed upon us that His word also says we should rejoice during every trial and tribulation.

This was the beginning of a long talk which we will try to share with you what we learned. His answer to our question as to whether to rejoice even during the storms in life was "especially then, especially now". We are His garden and we are to bring forth fruit in our life. Well any farmer knows that crap is just another word for fertilizer. We also know that fertilizer burns if there is no water and will ruin a crop quickly. How do we water it Lord? Water is often used in His word to refer to the Holy Spirit. Waters coming forth from inside us or the Living Water are used many times to talk of the Holy Spirit. Okay, so we need the Holy Spirit flowing to water this fertilizer in order to keep it from burning so we can bring forth fruit in our life. What is the best way to bring the Holy Spirit close and flowing in our marriage? Praise of course, is the best way! The Holy Spirit inhabits our praise! Okay, so the more fertilizer we have on our garden (or our life) the more water (or Living Water) we need in order to produce fruit! Yes Lord, now we understand why we are to praise you even in the storms of life, especially in the storms! Thank you Lord for sharing your heart and helping us to understand how now when we are going through the hurting it is the most important to praise you! You are so patient and loving with us and so worthy of our praise! Thank you Lord for all you do but mostly for who you ARE! You are indescribable and we are so very thankful for your love! Let our life be your garden and always let us be good soil to plant seeds in so that we may understand you more and share you with others! When we pray, "Give us this day our daily bread," we are, in a measure, shutting tomorrow out of our prayer. We do not live in tomorrow but in today. We do not seek tomorrow's grace or tomorrow's bread. They thrive best, and get most out of life, who live in the living present. They pray best who pray for today's needs, not for tomorrow's, which may render our prayers unnecessary and redundant by not existing at all!

True prayers are born of present trials and present needs. Bread, for today, is bread enough. Bread given for today is the strongest sort of pledge that there will be bread tomorrow. Victory today, is the assurance of victory tomorrow. Our prayers need to be focused upon the present, We must trust God today, and leave the morrow entirely with Him. The present is ours; the future belongs to God. Prayer is the task and duty of each recurring day— daily prayer for daily needs.
As every day demands its bread, so every day demands its prayer. No amount of praying, done today, will suffice for tomorrow's praying. On the other hand, no praying for tomorrow is of any great value to us today. To-day's manna is what we need; tomorrow God will see that our needs are supplied. This is the faith which God seeks to inspire. So leave tomorrow, with its cares, its needs, its troubles, in God's hands. There is no storing tomorrow's grace or tomorrow's praying; neither is there any laying-up of

today's grace, to meet tomorrow's necessities. We cannot have tomorrow's grace, we cannot eat tomorrow's bread, we cannot do tomorrow's praying. "Sufficient unto the day is the evil thereof;" and, most assuredly, if we possess faith, sufficient also, will be the good. God's message hasn't changed since the Old Testament—people will be judged for their unproductive lives.

God calls us to be active in our obedience. John compared people who claim they believe in God but don't live for him to unproductive trees that will be cut down. Just as a fruit tree is expected to bear fruit, God's people should produce a crop of good deeds. God has no use for people who call themselves Christians but do nothing about it. Like many people in John's day who were God's people in name only, we are of no value if we are Christians in name only. If others can't see our faith in the way we treat them, we may not be God's people at all. To be productive for God, we must obey his teachings, resist temptation, actively serve and help others, and share our faith. How productive are you for God?

CHAPTER 2

TRUST

Have I not commanded you? Be strong and of good
courage; do not be afraid, nor be dismayed, for the lord
your god is with you wherever you go." **Joshua 1:9 NKJV**

Confidence-The feeling or belief that one can rely on
someone or something; firm trust: reliability, fairness,
goodness, strength, benevolence, honesty and confident
expectation of something; hope.

Trust is a vital relationship concept that needs much
clarification.

T-Thanks- While they were eating, Jesus took some bread.
He thanked God and he broke the bread in pieces. Then he
gave it to his disciples. 'Take this and eat it', he said to
them. 'This is my body.'
v27 Then he took the cup of wine. He thanked God and he
offered the cup to them. 'All of you, drink from this', he
said. v28 'This is my blood to represent your new

agreement with God. I will pour out my blood so that he can forgive the sins of many people. v29 I am telling you the truth. I shall not drink wine again until I drink it with you where my Father rules.'
v30 Then they sang a song to God and they went out to the Mount of Olives. **Matt 26:27-30**

The author of Matthew was a Jewish Christian who wrote especially for Jews. One early Christian writer said, 'Matthew collected what Jesus taught in the Hebrew language.' This book contains much of what Jesus taught. So the early Christians gave Matthew's name to the whole book. Matthew collected taxes, but he became one of Jesus' 12 special friends (Matthew 9:9). Matthew did not write the first book about Jesus' life. Mark wrote about Jesus first. And Matthew uses much of what Mark wrote.

The Christian church put Matthew's book first because Matthew often refers to the Old Testament.
The head of a family thanked God before a meal. Jesus would probably have said the same prayer. 'Thank you, Lord our God. You are King of the world, and you bring food from the earth.' Jesus broke the bread in pieces and called it his body. This was a picture way to tell them about his death. He was telling them that he was going to die for them. He told them to take the bread. They must eat it. This showed that they accepted God's agreement. They were free to do so. God would forgive their sins because Jesus died.

They used four cups of wine at the Passover meal. These drinks reminded the Jews about the promises that God had made long ago. He had promised to rescue them from the country called Egypt. And he promised to make them his special people (Exodus 6:6-7). Jesus probably spoke at the time of the last cup of wine because they drank it at the end. Paul also wrote about this in 1 Corinthians 11:23-25. He said that Jesus took the cup 'after supper'. 'All' the disciples had to drink from the same cup of wine. That was to show their unity.

Jesus said that the wine represented his blood. It poured out from his body when he was on the cross. The relationship between God and Israel's people depended on how much they obeyed God's Law (Exodus 24:3-8). But Israel's people had broken that relationship. Jeremiah spoke about a new agreement (Jeremiah 31:31-34). An animal's blood represented 'the old agreement'.

When Jesus gave his life, he represented the new agreement. He made it possible for God to forgive people's sins. And that mends their relationship with God. Then people want to obey God. They realize how much he loves them. The old agreement had been just between God and the Jews. The new agreement is for 'many' people.

The Christian Church has always remembered what Jesus did at this special supper. They use bread and wine too. Different churches call it different names like: the Lord's Supper, the Eucharist, Holy Communion, the Breaking of Bread.

Jesus spoke about his death. But he knew that it was not

the end. He spoke about the time when he would drink wine with his disciples in the future. That would be where his Father rules. He knew that he would come to life again. At the Passover, Jews thanked God that he had made wine. So Jesus was using the picture language about the Messiah's special meal.

This song was one of the Psalms that they sang at special events. It may have been Psalm 118. Then they 'went out' from their worship. They went outside the city to the hill where olive trees grew. This was called the Mount of Olives. Jesus knew that he would soon be suffering.

R-Rejoice- -v1 Shout to the LORD, everyone that is righteous.

Verses 1 – 3: The word "shout" also means "sing" in Hebrew. Only God can make people righteous. It happens when he forgives them. "Forgive" means "GIVE our sin to Jesus to carry AWAY". Sin is doing wrong things. The psalm tells people to praise God with harp, lute and trumpet. Today we would probably use guitar, piano and trumpet. We can use any musical instrument to praise God. **Psalms 33:1**

U-Uphold- -v116 Give me help and life, as your word promises. And do not make me ashamed, because I hope in you. **Psalm 119:116**

S-Swift- Hear this, my dear brothers and sisters, we must all be careful to listen. We should only speak when we are sure that we are saying good things. We should not get angry easily. **James 1:19-v19**

James appeals to these Christians to listen to what he says to them. It is important for them to understand the truth of what he has written. It is important that they hear what he is going to say. They must always be ready to hear. They must listen to what God has to say to them. Then God will guide them. And he will give them the help that they need for their lives. They should listen and hear when other people speak. Then they may be able help them. Someone who talks all the time will not hear what other people say. It is important to be more willing to hear than to speak. They must not speak too much. They should think before they speak. They need to be sure that what they say is good and correct. They should not allow little things to make them angry. Anger will stop the mind receiving the truth of God. It will cause damage both to the one who is angry and to other people.

T-Trusts- Trust in the Lord. Here is the second precept, and one appropriate to the occasion. Faith cures fretting. Sight is cross-eyed, and views things only as they seem, hence her envy: faith has clearer optics to behold things as they really are, hence her peace. And do good. True faith is actively obedient. Doing good is a fine remedy for fretting. There is a joy in holy activity which drives away the rust of discontent. So shalt thou dwell in the land. In "the land" which floweth with milk and honey; the Canaan of the covenant. Thou shalt not wander in the wilderness of murmuring, but abide in the promised land of content and rest. "We which have believed do enter into rest." Very much of our outward depends upon the inward: where there is heaven in the heart there will be heaven in the house. And verily thou shalt be fed, or shepherded. To integrity and faith necessaries are guaranteed. The good shepherd will exercise his pastoral care over all believers. In truth they shall be fed, and fed on truth. The promise of God shall be their perpetual banquet; they shall neither lack in spirituals nor in temporals. Some read this as an exhortation, "Feed on truth; " certainly this is good cheer, and banishes for ever the hungry heart burnings of envy.

Marriage is not a test that you either pass or fail. It's an ongoing process of learning about each other and how to accommodate differences so that both of you can feel satisfied and grow in love for each other.
Marriage is also not a competition in which one person wins at the expense of the other. If both spouses are not happy with a decision, then the marriage suffers since one person's happiness cannot be at the expense of the other's. What are the qualities of trust? Then God remembered Rachel; he listened to her and opened her womb. She became pregnant and gave birth to a son and said, "God has taken away my disgrace."

Trust in your marriage almost always involves patience. Eventually God answered Rachel's prayers and gave her a child of her own. In the meantime, however, she had given her maidservant to Jacob. Trusting God is difficult when nothing seems to happen. But it is harder still to live with the consequences of taking matters into our own hands. Resist the temptation to think God has forgotten you.

Have patience and courage to wait for God to act. As the Egyptian army approached, the people of Israel saw them far in the distance, speeding after them, and they were terribly frightened and cried out to the Lord to help them. And they turned against Moses, whining, "Have you brought us out here to die in the desert because there were not enough graves for us in Egypt? Why did you make us leave Egypt?" **(Exodus 14:10-11)**

Trusting in your marriage often requires courage. Trapped against the sea, the Israelites faced the Egyptian army sweeping in for the kill. The Israelites thought they were doomed; after watching God's powerful hand deliver them from Egypt, their only response was fear, whining; and despair. Where was their trust in God? Israel had to learn from repeated experience that God was able to provide for them. God has preserved these examples in the Bible so that we can learn to trust him the first time. By focusing on God's faithfulness in the past, we can face crises with confidence rather than with fear and complaining. Trust in the LORD with all your heart and lean not on your own understanding; in all your ways acknowledge him, and he will make your paths straight. **(Proverbs 3:5-6)**

Trust in your marriage involves heartfelt confidence in God. Leaning has the sense of putting your whole weight on something, resting on and trusting in that person or thing. When we have an important decision to make, we sometimes feel that we can't trust anyone—not even God. But God knows what is best for us. You have to go with your instinct. And he knows even better than we do what we really want. We must trust him completely in every choice we make. We should not omit careful thinking or belittle our God-given ability to reason; but we should not trust our own ideas to the exclusion of all others. We must not be wise in our own eyes. We should always be willing to listen to and be corrected by God's Word and wise coaching. Bring your decisions to God in prayer, use the Bible as your guide, and follow God's leading. He will make your paths straight by both guiding and protecting you.

Trusting in your marriage includes giving God our future plans. To receive God's guidance, said Solomon, we must acknowledge God in all our ways. This means turning every area of life over to him. About a thousand years later, Jesus emphasized this same truth **(Matthew 6:33)**. Look at your values and priorities. What is important to you? In what areas have you not acknowledged him? What is his advice? In many areas of your life you may already acknowledge God, but it is the areas where you attempt to restrict or ignore his influence that will cause you grief. Make him a vital part of everything you do; then he will guide you because you will be working to accomplish his purposes. *But now God has shown us a different way to heaven—not by "being good enough" and trying to keep his laws, but by a new way (though not new, really, for the Scriptures told about it long ago). Now God says he will accept and acquit us—declare us "not guilty"—if we trust Jesus Christ to take away our sins. And we all can be saved in this same way, by coming to Christ, no matter who we are or what we have been like.* **(Romans 3:21-22)**

Trusting in your marriage is wholeheartedly believing in God's promises. after all this bad news about our sinfulness and God's condemnation, Paul gives the wonderful news. there is a way to be declared not guilty—by trusting Jesus Christ to take away our sins. Trusting means putting our confidence in Christ to forgive our sins, to make **in marriage** includes giving God our future plans. To receive God's guidance, said Solomon, we must acknowledge God in all our ways. This means turning every area of life over to him. About a thousand years later, Jesus emphasized this same truth **(Matthew 6:33)**. Look at your values and priorities. What is important to you? In what areas have you not acknowledged him? What is his advice? In many areas of your life you may already acknowledge God, but it is the areas where you attempt to restrict or ignore his influence that will cause you grief. Make him a vital part of everything you do; then he will guide you because you will be working to accomplish his purposes. *But now God has shown us a different way to heaven—not by "being good enough" and trying to keep his laws, but by a new way (though not new, really, for the Scriptures told about it long ago). Now God says he will accept and acquit us—declare us "not guilty"—if we trust Jesus Christ to take away our sins. And we all can be saved in this same way, by coming to Christ, no matter who we are or what we have been like.* **(Romans 3:21-22)**

Trust in your marriage is to permit to stay to the obligation and commitment. A position of trust; one upon which a person rely on. Trust is a key ingredient for a successful, happy marriage. Establishing trust with your husband/wife leads to more respect, love, commitment, communication and intimacy in your relationship. Without trust, you're more likely to jump to conclusions, get frustrated and angry and possibly even face a failed marriage. It's critical to build trust with your husband, whether you're establishing it in the initial stages of marriage or you're rebuilding it after it was destroyed.

Be yourself. Don't put on a front in any of your actions. When your wife/husband sees you frustrated, happy, tired or angry, it builds intimacy because it's the real you. Let your wife/husband take the reins in planning dates or vacations if he or she doesn't already. This shows that you trust them to make even minor decisions in your marriage.

Keep your promises. If you said you'll be somewhere at a certain time or do some-thing for your wife/husband, make sure you keep your word. Tell your wife/husband about any changes in your routine to avoid suspicion. If you're starting something new, such as hitting the gym regularly, tell him beforehand and explain why. Show a trustworthy attitude toward your wife/husband. Ask them if there is anything you have done that isn't trustworthy. It might be something that seems insignificant to you, such as a critical reaction when your spouse admits a weakness, but it erodes his trust in you. Also, ask him to point out any areas you need to work on to establish more trust. Tell the truth. Even a small lie is still a lie. This includes honesty in every area, including who you talk to, who you hang out with, where you spent money and what you talk about. Communicate, Communicate, Communicate often and honestly. Ask questions so there aren't any misunderstandings between the two of you. Listen to your husband's/wife's views and keep an open mind when he/she reveals their feelings.

Confide in your wife/husband. If you had a frustrating day at work or a disappointing conversation with a family member, friend, talk to him or her about it. If you're more open with your husband/wife, they are more likely to be open with you. Keep a great attitude in arguments. This means staying on topic, avoiding any insults and sticking to the facts. See a marital coach to help with any issues that might have led to broken trust. Avoid constantly bringing up the past, which only creates obstacles to establishing trust. Talk about accountability with each other, and discuss consequences for any broken trust in the future.

Chapter 3

HUMILITY

Pride goes before destruction, and a haughty spirit before stumbling. **Proverbs 16:18**

Trust in the LORD with all your heart and do not lean on your own understanding. In all your ways acknowledge Him, and He will make your paths straight. Do not be wise in your own eyes; fear the LORD and turn away from evil. It will be healing to your body and refreshment to your bone **Proverbs 3:5-8**

The quality of state of being humble; modest opinion of one's own importance of rank; meekness. A disposition to be humble; a lack of false pride.

*H-Hear-*Hear me when I call, O God of my righteousness! You have relieved me in *my* distress; Have mercy on me, and hear my prayer. **Psalms 4:1**

U-Unity- "Behold, how good and how pleasant it is for brethren to dwell together. Psalm 133:1

M-Marriage-- Marriage *is* honorable among all, and the
bed undefiled; but fornicators and adulterers God will
judge. Marriage is good and we should respect it. It is a
contract for life between a man and a woman. Sex in such a
marriage is pure and good. But it is wrong for either of
them to have sex with someone else. It is wrong for anyone
else to have sex with them. All acts of sex, other than in a
marriage, are sin. God will judge all who have wrong sex
with another person. **Hebrews13:4**

*I-Immovable-*Therefore, my beloved brethren, be
steadfast, immovable, always abounding in the work of the
Lord, knowing that your labor is not in vain in the Lord.

Paul ends by encouraging his Christian brothers and sisters.
They have the promise of the resurrection. So they should
not let anything disturb their faith. They should not let
anything destroy their faith. They should do all that they
can to work for Christ. Anything that they do for the Lord
will certainly be worthwhile. **1Corinthians15:58**

L-Lamp- "Or what woman, having ten silver coins, if she
loses one coin, does not light a lamp, sweep the house, and
search carefully until she finds *it?*[9] And when she has found
it, she calls *her* friends and neighbors together, saying,
'Rejoice with me, for I have found the piece which I lost!'

The silver coin may have been the woman's savings. One
coin was the amount of a day's wage. There is another

reason for its value. The 10 silver coins on a silver chain were the evidence that she was a married woman. She would wear them round her head, and nobody could take them from her. They were as precious as a wedding ring is today. In those days, the houses had tiny windows. This kept out the sun and heat. It was dark inside, so she would need to light a lamp. Then she could see where her coin had fallen.

I-Image- --[26] Then God said, "Let Us make man in Our image, according to Our likeness; let them have dominion over the fish of the sea, over the birds of the air, and over the cattle, over all the earth and over every creeping thing that creeps on the earth." [27] So God created man in His own image; in the image of God He created him; male and female He created them. **Genesis 1:26,27**

God created people to live **in** nature. Also, he created them to rule **over** nature. People are like animals in many ways. However, people are also different from animals. God made them special. God created people to be like himself. God said, 'Let every kind of animal grow on the earth.' But he specially 'created' people. People can love and they can think. They can know whether their behaviour is right or wrong. People wanted to know God and they wanted to obey him. Luke 15:8,9 God made people rulers over everything else that God had made. God said, 'Let **us** make people' because God consists of three persons. Those are the Father, Son and Holy Spirit. God is three persons in one God.

People as a 'true image like ourselves'. People (the man and the woman) were the only parts of God's creation that were like God himself. God did not create anything else that was like himself.

Let people 'rule'. God gave work to man. Also, God gave responsibility to him.

Verse 27 God 'created' people. Here the writer uses that special word again. God was kind to people. People are special to God.

People are images of God. This does not mean that man's body is like God. Man's body is like an animal. But man's spirit is like God. And so man can know God.

God said, 'Let us make people.' He did not say, 'I will make people.' Perhaps he said 'us' because he is 3 persons. He is the Father and the Son and the Holy Spirit. And he is also one God. But it is more likely that this is not the reason. The Hebrew word that means 'God' is like a plural word. Perhaps that is why God called himself 'we'.

God created people. To create means to make something that is completely new.

T-Two- Two are better than one,
Because they have a good reward for their labor. For if they fall, one will lift up his companion.
But woe to him who is alone when he falls, For he has no one to help him up.
[11] Again, if two lie down together, they will keep warm; But how can one be warm *alone?*

[12] Though one may be overpowered by another, two can withstand him.

And a threefold cord is not quickly broken. **Ecclesiastes 4:9-12**

Who can help each other in their labor?. Who can help each other when they fall?
Who can help each other withstand forces of opposition?

Y-Yesterday- [9] For we were born yesterday, and know nothing, Because our days on earth *are* a shadow. Job 8:9

What is Humility? The first point to understand is that humility is not self -abasement. to lower oneself is an indication, not of ego, but of preoccupation with self. True humility is self-forgetfulness. Forgetting about oneself. People are uniquely themselves. What is right for one person might be wrong for another. It might be spiritually helpful for some people but not for others; they might find it merely suppressive. People who are expansive by nature find it more relaxing to let their energy expand than by attempting to bottle it up. In expansion, however one must always hold the thought, that God is a doer".

One will not gain spiritually if what he tries to expand is his ego. so, what is it? how can we define humility? It is simply the willingness to be obedient to the will of the father, regardless of personal cost, and understand this; your humility will never depend on what men think of you, or what they say about you, that is irrelevant. Your humility has nothing to do with men s' opinions; and it's not based on their selfish sentiments. Does God put a requirement on

us that says of you're going to be humble, you can never
offend? John the Baptist lost his head, spoke the truth,
offended a woman, and lost his head. When the Pharisees
heard about it they probably celebrated; but in reality john
was standing for what was right; that's what God called him
to do; his obedience cost him everything, except early
entrance into the presence of God. Humility does not
speak about itself, out of the fullness of the heart, the
mouth speaks; it doesn't mean when your heart is full of
humility, you will keep on speaking how humble you are.
Humility gives encouragement to other people and put
others first and forgets about itself.

Humility in yourself and your marriage is an important
part of our spiritual life. Then Joshua tore his clothes and
fell face down to the ground before the ark of the LORD,
remaining there till evening. The elders of Israel did the
same, and sprinkled dust on their heads. **(Joshua 7:6)**
When our life falls apart, we also should turn to God for
direction and help. Like Joshua and the elders, we too
should often rely on our own skills and strength, especially
when the task before us seems easy. We go to God only
when the obstacles seem too great. However, only God
knows what lies ahead. Consulting him, even when we are
on a winning streak, may save us from grave mistakes or
misjudgments. God may want us to learn lessons, remove
pride, or consult others before he will work through us. We
need to humble ourselves so that we will be able to hear his
words. People today are just as eager to raise their social
status, whether by being with the right people, dressing for
success, living in a gated community or driving the right
car. Whom do you try to impress? Rather than aiming for
prestige, look for a place where you can humble yourself.
Some people try to give the appearance of humility in order

to manipulate others. Others think that humility means putting themselves down. Truly humble people compare themselves only with Christ, realize their sinfulness, and understand their limitations. On the other hand, they also recognize their gifts and strengths and are willing to use them as Christ directs. Humility is not self-degradation; it is a realistic assessment and commitment to serve. Naaman, a great hero, was used to getting respect, and he was outraged when Elisha treated him like an ordinary person. A proud man, he expected royal treatment. To wash in a great river would be one thing, but the Jordan was small and dirty. To wash in the Jordan, Naaman thought, was beneath a man of his position. But Naaman had to humble himself and obey Elisha's commands in order to be healed.

Humility in yourself and your marriage is the proper attitude before God. Joshua and the elders tore their clothing and sprinkled dust on their heads as signs of deep mourning before God. They were confused by their defeat at the small city of Ai after the spectacular Jericho victory, so they went before God in deep humility and sorrow to receive his instructions. When our life falls apart, we also should turn to God for direction and help. Like Joshua and the elders, we should humble ourselves so that we will be able to hear his voice.

Humility in yourself and your marriage keeps you from depending on our own strengths. When Joshua first went against Ai **(7:3)**, he did not consult God but relied on the strength of his army to defeat the small city. Only after Israel was defeated did they turn to God and ask what happened. Too often we rely on our own skills and strength, especially when the task before us seems easy. We go to God only when the obstacles seem too great.

However, only God knows what lies ahead. Consulting him, even when we are on a winning streak, may save us from great mistakes or misjudgments. God may want us to learn lessons, remove pride, or consult others before he will work through us.

Humility in yourself and your marriage makes our prayers direct and honest. So honest that we have to imagine praying the way Joshua prayed to God. This is not a formal church prayer; it is the prayer of a man who is afraid and confused by what is happening around him. Joshua poured out his real thoughts to God. Hiding your needs from God is ignoring the only one who can really help. God welcomes your honest prayers and wants you to express your true feelings to him. Any believer can become more honest in prayer by remembering that God is all-knowing and all-powerful and that his love is everlasting. But his officers tried to reason with him and said, "If the prophet had told you to do some great thing, wouldn't you have done it? So you should certainly obey him when he says simply to go and wash and be cured!" **(2 Kings 5:13)**

Humility in yourself and your marriage is good training in obedience. Naaman, a great hero, was used to getting respect, and he was outraged when Elisha treated him like an ordinary person. A proud man, he expected royal treatment. To wash in a great river would be one thing, but the Jordan was small and dirty. To wash in the Jordan, Naaman's thought, was beneath a man of his position. But Naaman had to humble himself and obey Elisha's commands in order to be healed.

Humility in yourself and your marriage clarifies our dependence on God. Obedience to God begins with humility. We must believe that his way is better than our own. We may not always understand his ways of working, but by humbly obeying, we will receive his blessings. We must remember that God's ways are best; God wants our obedience more than anything else; and God can use anything to accomplish his purposes.

Humility in yourself and your marriage challenges your pride. Naaman left in a rage because the cure for his disease seemed too simple. He was a hero, and he expected a heroic cure. Full of pride and self-will, he could not accept the simple cure of faith. Sometimes people react to God's offer of forgiveness in the same way. Just to believe in Jesus Christ somehow doesn't seem significant enough to bring eternal life. To obey God's commands doesn't seem heroic. What Naaman had to do to have his leprosy washed away is similar to what we must do to have our sin washed away—humbly accept God's mercy. Don't let your reaction to the way of faith keep you from the cure you need the most. When I consider your heavens, the work of your fingers, the moon and the stars, which you have set in place, what is man that you are mindful of him, the son of man that you care for him? **(Psalm 8:3-4)**

Humility is a deep awareness of unworthiness, not worthlessness. When we look at the vast expanse of creation, we wonder how God could be concerned for people who constantly disappoint him. Yet God created us only a little lower than himself or the angels! The next time you question your worth as a person, remember that God considers you highly valuable. We have great worth because we bear the stamp of the Creator. **(See Genesis 1:26-27)** For the extent of worth God places on all people.) Because

God has already declared how valuable we are to him, we can be set free from feelings of worthlessness.

Humility in yourself and your marriage increases our appreciation for God. To respect God's majesty, we must compare our self to his greatness. When we look at creation, we often feel small by comparison. To feel small is a healthy way to get back to reality, but God does not want us to dwell on our smallness. Humility means proper respect for God, not self-depreciation.

For everyone who tries to honor himself shall be humbled; and he who humbles himself shall be honored. **(Luke 14:11)**

 Humility in yourself and your marriage is essential for service to others. We have to serve others. Jesus advised people not to rush for the best places at a feast. People today are just as eager to raise their social status, whether by being with the right people, dressing for success, or wanting to hang around celebrities or buying a yacht, that they cannot afford. Whom do you try to impress? Rather than aiming for prestige, look for a place where you can serve. If God wants you to serve on a wider scale, he will invite you to take a higher place. Jesus Christ is our model for humility.

How can we humble ourselves? Some people try to give the appearance of humility in order to manipulate others. Others think that humility means putting themselves down. Truly humble people compare themselves only with Christ, realize their sinfulness, and understand their limitations. On the other hand, they also recognize their gifts and strengths and are willing to use them as Christ directs. Humility is not self-degradation; it is realistic assessment and commitment to serve. Humility in yourself and marriage is the ability to listen . Yes, we give them some attention but sometimes the words by our mouths are deflected by our hearts and minds-probably because of our pride.

Chapter 4

LOVE

L-lamp-Psalms 119:105-Your word *is* a lamp to my feet
And a light to my path.

Affections- A studied display of real or pretended feeling.
A feeling of strong attachment induced by that which
delights or commands admiration; preeminent ,kindness or
devotion to another; affection; tenderness; as the love of
brothers and sisters.

O-Overcome- And truly Jesus did many other signs in
the presence of His disciples, which are not written in
this book; [31] but these are written that you may believe
that Jesus is the Christ, the Son of God, and that
believing you may have life in His name. John 20:30,31
The purpose of John's Gospel. John wanted his
readers to believe 'that Jesus is the Messiah, God's
Son' (John 20:31). That is why he wrote his Gospel.
Matthew, Mark and Luke recorded many miracles in
their Gospels. But John chose to record only 7
miracles. He called them 'signs'. A sign is something
that gives evidence. The miracles gave evidence that
Jesus is God's Son..

John also emphasized that Jesus was human. John recorded
that Jesus was tired (John 4:6). John also recorded that

Jesus needed food (John 4:31). Jesus was very sad when his friend Lazarus died. At that time, Jesus cried (John 11:35). On another occasion, Jesus became angry with the people who did business in the Temple (John 2:15). And John also recorded that Jesus was thirsty (John 19:28).
Jesus was not half human and half God. He was completely human and completely God, too.

Many people agree that John emphasized this for a particular reason. In the early church, some people were teaching false beliefs about Jesus.
One group taught that Jesus was not really God. They said that he was just a man. They believed that the Holy Spirit entered him at his baptism. But before he died, the Holy Spirit left him. Another group taught that Jesus was not really a man. They said that he did not have a physical body. They believed that he was a spirit. And they believed that he only seemed to be human. Both these groups were wrong!
John and the other disciples had lived with Jesus for about three years. John knew that Jesus was a real man. Also John had seen the miracles that Jesus did. John watched Jesus die on a cross. And John had also seen Jesus after he (Jesus) had become alive again. John knew that Jesus had defeated death. And John had seen Jesus rise up to heaven.
So John knew that Jesus was a real man. But Jesus was and is also God's Son. John wrote his Gospel to prove this.

In many ways, John's Gospel is different from the other three Gospels. John did not include any stories about Jesus' birth or his baptism. John only recorded 7 miracles, which he called 'signs'. John did not include any parables (stories which Jesus told to teach something about God). But John recorded many long speeches that Jesus made.

The writer Eusebius (about AD 260-339) believed that
John knew about the other three Gospels. But when he
read them, John had not yet written his Gospel. He was
still just talking to people about his life with Jesus.

John agreed that the other Gospels were true accounts.
But Jesus was already preaching before King Herod put
John the Baptist in prison. The other Gospels did not
include an account of this. They recorded much about what
Jesus did in Galilee. Also, they recorded what Jesus did in
Jerusalem just before his death. But Jesus went to
Jerusalem at other times, too. So John provided the facts
that were missing from the other Gospels. He used
information that they did not have. John's account did not
disagree with the other Gospels. It added different
information, so that we can understand more about Jesus.

The second century writer, Clement, from Alexandria,
called John's Gospel a 'spiritual Gospel'. In some ways, he
was right. John did not record just facts about Jesus. John
had thought much about what Jesus had said. And John
had thought much about the miracles that he had seen. He
wanted to explain the spiritual meaning of Jesus' words and
acts.

But John also included many physical details. For example,
the loaves that Jesus used to feed 5000 people were 'barley
loaves' (John 6:9). He recorded the distance that the
disciples had travelled across the lake (John 6:19). And he
remembered how the smell of the perfume filled the house
at Bethany (John 11:32). These details do not seem
important. But they are memories of a person who was
present at these events. So John's Gospel is not just a
spiritual book. It is the personal account of someone who

had seen these events.

'Soon, after a short period of time, I will go away. Then you will not see me. But, soon after this, you will see me again.'

Jesus knew that, a few hours after this conversation, he would die. Then, the disciples would not be able to see him. But, three days later, he would show himself to the disciples. He would be alive again and they would see him.

V-Vows- When you promise to give a gift, think first! Proverbs 20:25

Otherwise, later you will be sorry. About the Proverbs (wise words) of Solomon (Proverbs 10:1 to Proverbs 22:16) The second major section in the Book of Proverbs is Proverbs 10:1, to Proverbs 22:16. This section contains 375 short poems. Most poems have two lines, and each poem is one verse long. Each poem is called a 'proverb'.
The structure of this section is unusual. Solomon did not separate the proverbs into groups. The proverbs change from one subject to another. However, their order does matter. Solomon uses an 'organic' (that is, 'natural') order. This order is similar to a conversation. For example, one proverb might explain the previous one. Another proverb might contrast with the previous one.
Together, these proverbs are like a conversation. Imagine that a group of wise people are talking about wisdom. Each person in the group speaks briefly. They all listen to each other. Then, each person tells his thoughts or ideas to the other people. The conversation would be similar to this

section of the Book of Proverbs.

Because of this structure, you cannot split these proverbs into smaller sections. Proverbs 10:1 to Proverbs 22:16 belong together. To help us to understand their meaning better.

The proverbs describe our lives. Often, they describe good things in our lives, for example, wisdom. Sometimes they describe bad things. They do not always explain whether something is good or bad. You need to use your own wisdom to decide. For example, Proverbs 10:15 says, 'Great wealth protects a rich man. Lack of wealth ruins a poor man.' This does not mean that we should try to get great wealth. Proverbs 8:10 told us that wisdom was better than wealth. Proverbs 10:15 describes our lives. We should want wisdom more than we want wealth.

These proverbs discuss many different subjects. However, all these subjects start with the first proverb. This proverb is about the difference between a wise son and a foolish son. The difference is (of course) wisdom.

Verse 25

Judges 11:30-40 explains this. Jephthah promised to kill and to give to God, whatever greeted him first. He expected an animal to greet him. However, his daughter greeted him. We should be careful about gifts and promises. It is better not to carry out a promise, than to do something evil. But you should not make a promise that you cannot carry out. See also Matthew 5:33-37.

E-Examine- A person should check his spiritual health before he shares the bread and the wine. 1Corinthian 11:28-v28

Paul's letters to Corinth

The 'previous' letter. Paul said, 'I wrote you a letter. In that letter, I told you to have nothing to do with men with bad character' (1 Corinthians 5:9). This letter is either lost or it may be in 2 Corinthians 6:14–7:1.

1 Corinthians. When Paul was in Ephesus, he received news about troubles in the church at Corinth. This news came from people who were living in Chloe's house (1 Corinthians 1:11), and from Stephanas, Fortunatus and Achaicus (1 Corinthians 16:17). A letter also came from the Christians in Corinth. They asked for Paul's advice about various problems. Paul wrote 1 Corinthians.

The second 'painful' visit. Paul heard that problems in Corinth were worse. So he made a second visit. There is no record about this. But Paul writes about when he visited Corinth for the 'third' time (2 Corinthians 12:14; 13:1-2). So there must have been a second visit.

The 'severe' letter. Paul's visit was not successful. So he wrote a letter when he was feeling very hurt (2 Corinthians 2:4). He was almost sorry that he had sent it. Some writers believe that chapters 10-13 in 2 Corinthians are the 'severe' letter.

The letter to show that the Christians at Corinth and Paul were friends again. Paul was so worried about his 'severe' letter that he went to meet Titus. Titus had taken the severe letter to Corinth. Paul met Titus in Macedonia and learned that all was well. So, he wrote chapters 1-9 in 2 Corinthians. It is possible that someone put the severe letter and the next letter together in the wrong order.

A Christian eats the bread and drinks the wine. He must prepare himself before he does that. He must not forget that he is part of the body of Christ. The body of Christ is the church. Christ's death was an act of love. Therefore, the members of his body, the church, must show love to each other. If they do not, God will judge them.

Loving yourself and others

Love is many different things to many different people. The number of definitions is almost endless. Think about how you define love and how you know when you "are in love." Not in lust with someone.
When a person has made his ultimate goal to love another, then no matter what is needed it will be done. Basically, a husband says in his heart, that no part of my life is more important than my commitment to care for my wife. This is where God's genuine love is implanted in our hearts.

Beloved let us love one another, for love is of God; and everyone who loves is born of God and knows God. He who does not love does not know God, for God is love. In this the love of God was manifested toward us, that God has sent His only begotten Son into this world, that we might live through Him. In this is love, not that we loved God, but that He loved us and sent His Son to be the propitiation of our sins. Beloved, if God so loved us, we also ought to love one another.
1 John 4:7-11 NKJV

God's love in yourself and marriage? well, in the same way heaven will be happier over one lost sinner who returns to God than over ninety-nine others who haven't strayed away! **(luke 15:7)**
God's love is forgiving. We may be able to understand a God who would forgive sinners who come to him for mercy, but a God who tenderly searches for sinners and

then joyfully forgives them must possess an extraordinary love! This is the kind of love that prompted Jesus to come to earth to search for lost people and save them. This is the kind of extraordinary love that God has for you. If you feel far from God, don't despair he is searching for you. For I am convinced that neither death nor life, neither angels nor demons, neither the present nor let us love one another, for love is of God; and everyone who loves is born of God and knows God. He who does not love does not know God, for God is love. In this the love of God was manifested toward us, that God has sent His only begotten Son into this world, that we might live through Him. In this is love, not that we loved God, but that He loved us and sent His Son to be the propitiation of our sins. Beloved, if God so loved us, we also ought to love one another.
1 John 4:7-11 NKJV

God's love in yourself and marriage? well, in the same way heaven will be happier over one lost sinner who returns to God than over ninety-nine others who haven't strayed away! **(luke 15:7)**

 God's love is forgiving. we may be able to understand a God who would forgive sinners who come to him for mercy. but a God who tenderly searches for sinners and then joyfully forgives them must possess an extraordinary love! This is the kind of love that prompted Jesus to come to earth to search for lost people and save them. This is the kind of extraordinary love that God has for you. If you feel far from God, don't despair he is searching for you. for I am convinced that neither death nor life, neither angels nor demons, neither the present nor the future, nor any powers, neither height nor depth, nor anything else in all creation, will be able to separate us from the love of God that is in Christ Jesus our Lord. **(Romans 8:38-39)**

God's love in marriage is beyond measure. These words were written to a church that would soon undergo terrible persecution. In just a few years, Paul's hypothetical situations would turn into painful realities. This passage reaffirms God's profound love for his people. No matter what happens to us, no matter where we are, we can never be lost to his love. Suffering, Trials and Tribulations should not drive us away from God; it should help us to identify with him further and allow his love to reach us and heal us.

This is the kind of love that prompted Jesus to come to earth to search for lost people and save them. This is the kind of extraordinary love that God has for you. If you feel far from God, don't despair. He is searching for you. Yes, you! Suffering, Trials and Tribulations should not drive us away from God; it should help us to identify with him further and allow his love to reach us and heal us. God paid dearly with the life of his Son, the highest price he could pay. Jesus accepted our punishment, paid the price for our sins, and then offered us the new life that he had bought for us.

When we share the gospel with others, our love must be like Jesus'. We must be willing to give up our own comfort and security so that others might join us. Our society confuses love and lust. Unlike lust, God's kind of love is directed outward toward others, not inward toward ourselves. It is utterly unselfish. This kind of love goes against our natural inclinations. It is possible to practice this love only if God helps us set aside our own desires and instincts, so that we can give love while expecting nothing in return. Thus the more we become like Christ, the more love we will show to others. God's Love is the key to walking in the light, because we cannot grow spiritually while we hate others. Our growing relationship with God will result in growing relationships. When we are wronged, often our first reaction is to get even. Instead, Jesus said we should do good to those who wrong us!

Our desire should not be to keep score, but to love not let them rule your thoughts, decisions, and actions. When you are uncertain about what to do, ask yourself which course of action best demonstrates love for God and love for others. In the battle to maintain sound teaching and moral and doctrinal purity, it is possible to lose a charitable spirit. Prolonged conflict can weaken or destroy our patience and affection. In defending the faith, guard against any structure or rigidity that weakens love.

God's love in yourself and marriage is eternal. Believers have always had to face hardships in many forms. Persecution, illness, imprisonment, even death. These could cause them to fear that they have been abandoned by Christ. But Paul exclaims that it is impossible to be separated from Christ. His death for us is proof of his unconquerable love. Nothing can stop Christ's constant presence with us. God tells us how great his love is so that we will feel totally secure in him. If we believe these overwhelming assurances, we will not be afraid. For God so loved the world that he gave his one and only Son, that whoever believes in him shall not perish but have eternal life. **(John 3:16)**
God's love in yourself and marriage is sacrificial. The entire gospel comes to a focus in the verse below. God's love is not static or self-centered; it reaches out and draws others

in. Here God sets the pattern of true love, the basis for all love relationships—when you love someone dearly, you are willing to pay dearly for that person's responsive love. God paid dearly with the life of his Son, the highest price he could pay. Jesus accepted our punishment, paid the price for our sins, and then offered us the new life that he had bought for us. When we share the gospel with others, our love must be like Jesus'. We must be willing to give up our own comfort and security so that others might join us in receiving God's love. Give thanks to the LORD, for he is good. His love endures forever. **(Psalm 136:1)**

God's love in yourself and marriage is inexhaustible. repeated throughout this psalm is the phrase, "His love endures forever." This psalm may have been a responsive reading, with the congregation saying these words in unison after each sentence. The repetition made this important lesson sink in. God's love includes aspects of love, kindness, mercy, and faithfulness. We never have to worry that God will run out of love, because it flows from a well that will never run dry.

God's love is very patient and kind, never jealous or envious, never boastful or proud, never haughty or selfish or rude. God's love does not demand its own way. It is not irritable or touchy. It does not hold grudges and will hardly even notice when others do it wrong. It is never glad about injustice, but rejoices whenever truth wins out. If you love someone you will be loyal to him no matter what the cost. You will always believe in him, always expect the best of him, and always stand your ground in defending him. **(1 Corinthians 13:4-7)**

Love is more important than spiritual gifts. Love is more important than all the spiritual gifts exercised in the church body. Great faith, acts of dedication or sacrifice, and miracle-working power produce very little without love. Love makes our actions and gifts useful. Although people have different gifts, love is available to everyone. Love benefits others. our society confuses love and lust. Unlike lust, God's kind of love is directed outward toward others, not inward toward ourselves. It is utterly unselfish. This kind of love goes against our natural inclinations. It is possible to practice this love only if God helps us set aside our own desires and instincts, so that we can give love while expecting nothing in return. Thus the more we become like Christ, the more love we will show to others.

Dear brothers, I am not writing out a new rule for you to obey, for it is an old one you have always had, right from the start. You have heard it all before. Yet it is always new, and works for you just as it did for Christ; and as we obey this commandment, to love one another, the darkness in our lives disappears and the new light of life in Christ shines in. **(1 John 2:7-8)**

Love is a command. The commandment to love others is both old and new. It is old because it comes from the old testament **(Leviticus 19:18)**. It is new because Jesus interpreted it in a radically new way **(John 13:34-35)**. In the Christian church, love is not only expressed by showing respect; it is also expressed through self-sacrifice and servant hood **(john 15:13)**. In fact, it can be defined as **"selfless giving,"** reaching beyond friends, and family to enemies and persecutors **(Matthew 5:43-48)**. Love should be the unifying force and the identifying mark of the Christian community. Love is the key to walking in the light, because we cannot grow spiritually while we hate others. Our growing relationship with god will result in growing relationships with others. Love is a choice. Does this mean that if you dislike someone you aren't a Christian? These verses are not talking about disliking a disagreeable Christian brother or sister. There will always be people we will not like as well as others. John's words focus on the attitude that causes us to ignore or despise others, to treat them as irritants, competitors, or enemies. Christian love is not a feeling, but a choice. We can choose to be concerned with people's well-being and treat them with respect, whether or not we feel affection toward them. If we choose to love others, God will help us express our love. **There is a saying, "Love your friends and hate your enemies." But I say: Love your enemies! Pray for those who persecute you! (Matthew 5:43,)**

Love in yourself and your marriage should choose forgiveness rather than revenge. Forgiveness is renunciation or cessation of resentment, indignation or anger as a result of a perceived offense, disagreement, or mistake, or ceasing to demand punishment or restitution. The act of excusing a mistake or offense; in other words; readiness to forgive. When we are wronged, often our first reaction is to get even. Instead, Jesus said we should do good to those who wrong us! Our desire should not be to keep score, but to love and forgive. This is not natural—it is supernatural. Only God can give us the strength to love as he does instead of planning vengeance, pray for those who hurt you.

How can we love God? "The most important one," answered Jesus, "is this: 'Hear, O Israel, the Lord our God, the Lord is one. Love the Lord your God with all your heart and with all your soul and with all your mind and with all your strength.' The second is this: 'Love your neighbor as yourself.' There is no commandment greater than these." **(Mark 12:29-31)**

Loving God is the greatest human act. God's laws are not burdensome. They can be reduced to two simple principles: love God and love others. These commands are from the Old Testament **(Deuteronomy 6:5;Leviticus 19:18)**. When you love God completely and care for others as you care for yourself, then you have fulfilled the intent of the Ten Commandments and the other Old Testament laws. According to Jesus, these two commandments summarize all of God's laws. Let them rule your mind, heart and actions. A mind is the product of mental activity; that which one thinks, consideration, attention, care or regard. The heart is the act or process of deciding to make up one's mind. Actions are something that is done or performed. An exertion of power or force. When you are uncertain about what to do, ask yourself which course of action best demonstrates love for God and love for others. Once more he asked him, "Simon, son of John, are you even my friend?" Peter was grieved at the way Jesus asked the question this third time. "Lord, you know my heart; you know I am," he said. Jesus said, "Then feed my little sheep." **(John 21:17)**

Loving God means serving him. Jesus led peter through an experience that would remove the cloud of his denial. Peter had disowned Jesus three times. Three times Jesus asked Peter if he loved him. When Peter answered yes, Jesus told him to feed his sheep. It is one thing to say you love Jesus, but the real test is willingness to serve him. Peter had repented, and here Jesus was asking him to commit his life.

Peter's life changed when he finally realized who Jesus was. His occupation changed from fisherman to evangelist; his identity changed from impetuous to "rock"; and his relationship to Jesus changed—he was forgiven, and he finally understood the significance of Jesus' words about his death and resurrection.

Loving god requires everything we have and who we are. Jesus asked peter three times if he loved him. the first time Jesus said, "do you truly love **[greek** agape: volitional, self-sacrificial love] me more than these?" the second time, Jesus focused on peter alone and still used the word translated from the **greek word** agape. the third time, Jesus used the word translated from the **greek word** phileo (signifying affection, affinity, or brotherly love) and asked, in effect, "are you even my friend?" wow! how profound is this. each time peter responded with the word translated into **greek as** phileo. Jesus doesn't settle for quick, superficial answers. He has a way of getting to the heart of the matter. Peter had to face his true feelings and motives when Jesus confronted him. How would you respond if Jesus asked you, "Do you truly love me?" Do you really love Jesus? Are you even his friend? Yet there is one thing wrong; you don't love me as at first! Think about those times of your first love (how different now!) Nevertheless I have somewhat against thee, because thou hast left thy first love. Remember therefore from whence thou art fallen, and repent, and do the first works; or else I will come unto thee quickly, and will remove thy candlestick out of his place, except thou repent. **(Revelation 2:4-5)**

Loving god, yourself and marriage must guide everything else we do. Christ commended the church at Ephesus for working hard, persevering, resisting sin, critically examining the claims of false apostles, and enduring hardships without becoming weary. Every church should have these characteristics, but these good efforts should spring from our love for Jesus Christ. Both Jesus and John stressed love for one another as an authentic proof of the gospel **(John 13:34;1 John 3:18-19)**. In the battle to maintain sound teaching and moral and doctrinal purity, it is possible to lose a charitable and righteous spirit. Prolonged conflict can weaken or destroy our patience and affection. in defending the faith, guard against any structure or rigidity that weakens your love for god expressing love for yourself and in your marriage.

"All the paths of the lord are steadfast, love and faithfulness." **Psalms 25:10**

Saying "I love you with hearts of love. The words I love you may seem overused by some but when we speak them to each other, we say them with all the conviction of our hearts. In our words of love, we want each other to hear the strength of our commitment and to be comforted by how much we care. Our love may not be a tangible gift, but it is a source of powerful support for each other. The power in love strengthens us so that we believe the two of us can overcome anything and for each other fills us with a joy that can never be extinguished.

When all is said and done, we rely on love to guide us through. We want to give 100 percent in all that we do with each other. We do so with joy in our hearts. We have received god's constant care and love whether a situation is defined as the aggregate of biological, psychological, and socio cultural factors acting on an individual to condition behavioral patterns. No matter what you have been through; death of a child, parent, spouse, losing material things, health, etc; with god's love and protection you can overcome. Our love for god, self; whether we are evil or good. We live in god's love. No one can deny it. Yes, we might go through hard times, but in the end we all will be accountable on how we responded to god's daily care for our lives. Not one of us will be able to say that god has not provided for us. God's rule of love is not dependent on our inherent goodness or outward activities.

"But I say to you, love your enemies, and pray for those who persecute you in order that you may be sons of your father who is in heaven; for He causes his sun to rise on the evil and the good, and sends rain on the righteous and the unrighteous. **(Matthew 5:44-45)**

Because of this provision of love, we are expected to reflect this kind care for others by the way we treat others. God's love is perfect and awesome.. We are responsible to treat one another with love, faith, humility and trust. God did not just love the righteous, and so we too are to love all. For if you love those who love you, what reward have you? Do not even the tax-gatherers do the same? "And if you greet your brothers only, what do you do more than others? Do not even the Gentiles do the same? "Therefore you are to be perfect, as your heavenly Father is perfect. **(Matthew 5:46-48)**.

Because of god's love he created us and allowed us to participate in his own image. Since, god is love **(1 john 4:16)** he gave man and woman the capacity to love. Man and woman were made with the ability to love God and to love each other. In order to express that love fully there must be an alternative. God wants us to fellowship with Him, not because we have no other choice, but because it is our choice. We have to hear God's voice every day. We are not trying to get to super spiritual here; but who made the heavens and the earth; the oceans that his hands are holding back. God will not force man to love Him. Love does not work that way. Love waits and love permits ; the other the freedom to respond out of a desire to do so. In the Garden of Eden , God wanted man to remain in unity; however, he provided an alternative. That alternative was the one forbidden tree. To eat from it would be disobedience and disobedience would break the ideal fellowship. When Adam and Eve chose that alternative they hid from God **(Genesis 3:8)** They had to leave the garden and be separated from God **(Genesis 3:24)** Are you hiding from God? and what's in your garden? We often call the tree of knowledge of good and evil man's temptation but we like to call it the master gardener.

As long as Adam and eve did not partake of the tree, they were saying to god , "father we are here because we want to be and because we love you, not because we have to be here. They had the opportunity to show and preserve their fellowship with god, but their sin broke the unity. Sin is turning to our own way . Our own way is what will get us into deeper sin and out of the will of god. "all we like sheep have gone astray; we have turned everyone to his own way" **(Isaiah 53:6)** God's love permitted the temptation because out of His love He made us in His own image. Out of true love he gave us the gift of freedom. He did not force the one and only decision on man but He did force man to the position of making a choice. What choice will you make today?

'Love in ourselves and marriages helps us see that 'love' is the key to a great marriage by always working, working, working and never failing. In **1 Corinthians 13:4-8.** The description of love is not a simple monument but a clear testimony of the most powerful force on earth. When we choose to give up and choose others than love, we simply are allowing the darkness of the world to seize our marriage. God's love, however, can take any devastating and dark situation, turn it around and bring God's light to shine. This is what God did with Jesus Christ. Read how the darkness cannot be overcome with darkness. "The light still shines in the darkness and the darkness has never put it out" **(John 1:5).**

The same is true with God's powerful force of love. Notice how faith , love trust, humility are joined together. "By this we know that we love the children of God, when we love God and observe His commandments. For this is the love of God, that we keep His commandments; and His commandments are not burdensome. For whatever is born of God overcomes the world; and this is the victory that has overcome the world--our faith. And who is the one who overcomes the world, but he who believes that Jesus is the Son of God?" **(1 John 5:2-5).** God has created each of His children to be a conduit of His love. A channel through which anything is conveyed. There is no grander place for this to be seen than in marriage. Wherever God's love comes down and touches a heart, the center of the total personality; people are changed for the good. It may take years; but yes God can do it. We can see this when Jesus mingled with the people when walking through their towns. They loved Him. They felt his heart. We will also see the same things happen when a husband or wife opens up their heart and love his or her spouse.

Shortly after the weddings and honeymoon; many couples are soon convinced that there is no real such thing as love. Their faith in love has been shipwrecked in disappointment. So what happened? Simply; they need to get to know and respect one another. We should first acknowledge that they had lust and never really had genuine love. Lust is an intense sexual desire or appetite, uncontrolled or illicit sexual desire, a passionate or overwhelming desire or craving. Love is true. God's love keeps steadfast right through all the ups and downs. The love that fails is rooted in self and cannot stand the tests of daily life issues. True love is found only in God's love. God has somehow worked within us some instinctive sense of sacrifice and goodness that works in a very limited way. We need to look deeper for a divine love to sustain marriage.

Where can we find this love? It is in the heart and the soul of the individual that truly want marriage.
Jesus came to show us God's love in action. Christ's death shows us the way He cared for people. As a result, those that repent and follow Him are able to live in that full love. To choose love is to respond to God. When God's love is in our relationships, special things occur. As spouses we need to be committed to bringing God's love to our mates. We need to be strategic. Although husbands are especially commanded by God to love their wives, As believers, we need to walk closely with God to get that love. Only His love can help us through difficult relationship problems. Love helps us to have the proper personal motivation. All through the gospels Jesus regularly took time to be alone with His Father. This enabled Him to be a vessel that

His Heavenly Father used to bring His love and healing to people. In a similar way, we need to meet regularly with God to know how best we can show God's love to our spouse. Let us share a story with you about a practical way to show God's love.

"For a while we were still helpless, at the right time Christ died for the ungodly. For one will hardly die for a righteous man; though perhaps for the good man someone would dare even to die. But God demonstrates His own love toward us, in that while we were yet sinners, Christ died for us" (**Romans 5:6-8**).

The people he helped are called helpless, ungodly and sinners. Helpless means deprived of strength, powerless, and incapacitated. The ungodly are those that do not accept God, atheistic or a particular religious doctrine. The sinner's are wicked, impious and one who sins; but God's love was great enough to help the unkind, mean and downright evil people. The help God provided was the life of His only Son, Jesus Christ. The wedding is where each partner commits themselves to live out their sacrificial love. The marriage and the vows is where each partner seeks God for His love to shine through their lives into the lives of his or her spouse. Let us give you an example of the wedding vows for man and woman. I, Jerome Moore take you Ivy Moore to be my wedded wife. To have and to hold, From this day forward, for better or for worse, for richer or poor, in sickness or in health, to love and cherish until death do us part. With deepest joy I receive you into my life that together we may be as one. As is Christ to His body, the church, so I will be to you a loving and faithful husband/wife. Always will I perform my headship over you even as Christ does over me, knowing that His Lordship is one of the holiest desires for my life. I promise you my deepest love, my fullest devotion, my tender care. I promise I will live first unto God rather than others or even you. I promise that I will lead our lives into a life of faith and hope in Christ Jesus. Ever honoring God's guidance by His spirit through the Word, And so throughout life, no matter what may lie ahead of us, I pledge to you my life as a loving and faithful husband. I will take you to be my wedded wife. Many people are trained to act kindly. Each society has rules of politeness. Love is kind and those that live out these common courtesies bring a special blessing into their marriages. They in fact are living out God's principles of love, but it is important not to confuse this with God's love. Good training and wisdom is necessary, but it should not be our end. It will never bring that kind of commitment that marriages demand.

God's love is a heart change that shapes a person's desire to care for the other person more than himself. God's love motivates a person to act kindly in situations that go far beyond those areas that typical polite rules would call one to observe.
Many other people just don't have that training. This is absolutely tragic.
This is where Anger, Bitterness, Hatred, Jealousy, Envy, and Strife set in.
When a person has made his ultimate goal to love another, then no matter what is needed, it will be done. He is willing to die for the other. Basically, a husband says in his heart, that no part of my life is more important than my commitment to care for my wife, my helper, my love, my soul mate, my companion & my queen. This is where God's genuine love is implanted in our hearts.

Today's generation is getting more and more reluctant to getting married. A recent re-port cited that half of all women by the age of 30 have lived with a partner outside of marriage. You have probably heard the story. "I don't want to live through what my parents did!" They did not witness their parents' courtship and wedding day. The memories of their parents fighting each other stain their poor minds. They know more of anger and hatred than love. They simply do not choose marriage. It no longer is an alternative. They haven't found love, and have lost complete hope in marriage. And guess what?! Their parents aren't debating with them! Many of these same parents are allowing their daughter's boyfriend to live in their house!

There are two kinds of love: human love and divine love. They both come from God but differ on an essential point which will be discussed later. Most people think they understand love. They don't. They know only of the limited kind of love – human love. Indeed it is a greatly limited version never designed to fully satisfy. This is like those sample computer programs that allow you to operate only certain functions.
They do not work perfectly; they never were meant to. In fact, the sample program was not designed to use but to encourage a person to upgrade to the full application with all of its features. This is the way it is with God's love commonly found in the world. This is what we call human love.

We would be greatly mistaken to think that this limited version of love is all there is to life. However, many people are building their marriages and making long term commitments with only this limited kind of love. This is a shame, especially considering how true love makes beautiful relationships. We want you to better understand the purposes of this limited kind of love which God has given to mankind too. If it was not for this kind of love, our world would not be at all a nice place to live. This kind of love is not bad but limited. Human love was designed to cause us to seek for genuine love in all of its richness. Let's look at three instances of this limited version of love.

Love between man and woman

This love beautifully illustrates how a man and woman can become caught in the joy of serving the needs of the other. They are willing to share everything. They can't be apart. Every free moment they talk with each other. It is often called infatuation while some call it 'puppy love.'
"Your oils have a pleasing fragrance, Your name is like purified oil; Therefore the maidens love you" (Song of Solomon 1:3).

There are depraved forms of these relationships when sexual passion is released or when gifts and time are only a ploy to manipulate and use the other. When, however, the bridle of lust is kept under control, friendships and relationships can grow quickly and deeply. The guy buys gifts for his loved one simply because he loves her. It greatly pleases him to have her by his side.
However, we only need to enter into one of their arguments to see how superficial this kind of love can be. He usually treats her special, but not during these times! He becomes angry and bitter. One wonders how things could change so drastically. Simple misunderstandings are heated up to full blown arguments just because they do not have the patience to listen carefully to each other. Though the man-woman love is special, it points to the need of a greater love.

We only can meet up with true love when we meet up with God. One cannot find love anywhere else except in knowing God for "God is love." We should not look for love in man but in God. When we discover this love in man, we must not stop there. Man will disappoint, but God never will.

Love by definition is a constant stream of sacrificial and devoted acts toward another. In summary, love at least must have two elements to be true love. To the degree human love carries out these tasks, the more it is shaped by the divine hand.

Love is focused. **Paul in 1 Corinthians 13** describes love as "... patient, love is kind, ... love does not brag and is not arrogant." Love's beauty is not found in the way it compromises what is best for what is inferior, but in the way it demonstrates its giving nature.

We love, because He first loved us. **(1 John 4:19).** Love excels in what we find most difficult to do waiting rather than demanding; extending tender care to obstinate people; determining to fulfill the needs of others at cost to one's own needs and desires; acknowledgement of our weaknesses rather than clamoring for compliments.

Many today think the ideal marriage is 50/50, the perfect compromise. God intends the marriage to be 100/100, where each spouse gives his or her total self to each other. Genuine love goes out of his way to patiently, kindly and humbly treat each other. True love is not giving less than what is demanded, but it is the total giving of oneself to rightly care for the other. This is the sacrificial aspect seen above in the three examples but carried out in every situation. God's love does not stop here though.

Lastly, love by definition 'does not stop.' Love "bears all things, believes all things, hopes all things, endures all things." No 'thing' can or will stop true love. Love is not a feeling though it produces many wonderful feelings. Love is above all a commitment to unreservedly give of oneself to another. If love stops, then we know it was not divine love. If love finds barriers with a person's personality, peculiarities, looks or gifts, then we must conclude that our love was merely a form of enchantment or lust.

Love is easier when both are in good health, prosperous, vigorous, young and beautiful, but time brings challenges with it in the form of sickness, weakness, getting old, etc. Genuine love never fails because it does not give up; it can not give up. Love's strength is not derived from what a person sees in another but by ones commitment to that person. Love demands every last drop of selfishness. Real love doesn't stop with the struggles of life but grows in a fuller way as one stands in God's presence.
Love is not ignorant of the troubles, the pain, the hurt, and the shame that is present or threatened, for it is in these very circumstances that love grows stronger. Many people want to get out of marriage when facing great difficulties. This is not true love. Genuine love follows God into eternity.

Although many people would claim to love, only a few have been seized by its magnificent power, insight and commitment. We see the shallowness of people's commitments when those who take their marriage vows state that they will stay married "as long as we both shall love". Truly, they don't have any notion of what true love is. The true marriage vow states, "As long as we both shall live." Love by definition has many components, without them, it is something other than love.

Love is patient, love is kind, and is not jealous; love does not brag and is not arrogant, does not act unbecomingly; it does not seek its own, is not provoked, does not take into account a wrong suffered, does not rejoice in unrighteousness, but rejoices with the truth; bears all things, believes all things, hopes all things, endures all things. Love never fails; remember when you feel like giving up that God's love is not just modeled in Christ's life but has been brought right into your own lives and marriage as followers of Christ. And so Christ commands us to love one another as God has loved us. Some say it is hardest to love those who are closest. I'm not sure about this, but we do know that if you are faithful in loving with His love: unselfishly, kindly, patiently and persistently, that your love which is from God will usher you two into the most beautiful relationship possible on earth.

May God Richly Bless You With His Love

Dear God, I have been so filled with bitterness, hate and malicious talk that I have been poisoning those around me with evil. I have sinned against You. You are light and love; I am darkness and selfishness. I just don't know how to love. I heard that you can give some love to me. I need it real bad. I need you to teach me about love. I need you to plant it deep down in my soul. I want your love to ignite my soul. I also want to be your vessel of love. I know this will not be easy. Those around me are bad enough. But I have made things worse with my evil touch. I want to be changed by You, Lord. I want you to empower me to live to love. Yes, I know it is very different than I now experience. But that is the fact I now face. I don't want my life with all its hatred. I want what your love and peace. So Heavenly God, come save this wretched soul. Change me. Forgive **me**. Let the love of God as seen in Jesus Christ live in me. I accept Jesus Christ to be the one who cleanses me of all my sin. I accept Jesus Christ as my Lord who will direct my paths into Your love. Lead me forth for your glory and for the sake of those around me. In Jesus Christ We pray, **Amen.**

As we have Prayed together everyday together and interceded on the behalf of marriages and others and trusted in the Lord that we could, we can, and we did complete this book of The Power of 4 in Your Marriage; we trusted God for the revelation that was given to us and that the person that we trust; trust us and the person that we love the most loves us. The gift to see couples move from the natural to the supernatural of one flesh, one mind; and one soul. It is not going to be an easy task but with the Lord on our side and keeping Him in our life every minute; we can fulfill the calling, the gifts and purpose in life.

May God richly bless you with His Love?

Salvation is the beginning of a new life with God. This is only the beginning of a wonderful growing relationship with God. Read His Word and join His people in prayer. God has a lot to teach you on being His agent of love. Once God's love is in us, we can take some important steps to grow in our love for our spouse.
If you have not accepted Jesus in your life as your personal savior you may do so today! The Bible says, "That if thou shalt confess with thy mouth the Lord Jesus, and shalt believe in thine heart that God hath raised Him from the

dead, thou shalt be saved" (Romans 10:9).

Pray this prayer from your heart today! "Dear Jesus, I believe that you died for me and rose again on the third day. I confess I am a sinner...I need your love and forgiveness... Come into my heart. Forgive my sins. I receive your eternal life...
Confirm your love by giving me peace, joy and supernatural love for others. Amen.

□**Yes, Marriage** Coaches & Pastors Jerome & Ivy!

I made a decision to accept Christ as my personal Savior today. Please send me my free gift to help me with my new life in Christ.

_____

Name

_____

_____

Address

_____

City State Zip

_____

Phone Email

_____

_____

Birthday
Anniversary

Email the information to:<ins>marriage4lifeinstitute@gmail.com</ins>
You should receive your gift within 2-3weeks.

To know more on the chapters that we have discussed and the books that we have written; please check our schedule often and join us for workshops and seminars coming to your area soon.

Last but not least seek counsel. In Proverbs 13:20, the Bible states the importance of seeking the advice of wise individuals. If you or your mate are struggling with any of the issues discussed in this book, be willing to get the professional help you need.

Depending on the problem, this help can come from Marital Coaches & Pastors Jerome & Ivy Moore. "It's best to seek mentor ship as soon as you start having problems, rather than wait until they become a breaking point. marriage4lifeinstitute@gmail.com
www.marriage4lifeinstitute.com

ABOUT THE AUTHORS

Relationship Guru's & Pastors Jerome & Ivy Moore are CEO's of Marriage for Life Institute, Orlando, Florida. They are respected leaders and teachers in the word of God. Their leadership style is teaching effectively to couples and touching hundreds of souls every week through; weekly radio programs, social media, workshops, seminars and face to face with private mentoring programs. They have written one other book besides this one entitled Igniting the Flame of One (building marriages; educating couples). Their heart has always been for couples to restore, repair, renew and rebuild broken relationships. They have been married for 29 years and have 2 children and one grandson.

Made in the USA
Middletown, DE
21 May 2022

66058203R00050